Basix

Scales and Modes

Steve Hall/Ron Manus

Get Down to BASIX™!

BASIX™ is all you need to take off with your instrument. Alfred has worked hard to help you begin learning today with our easy-to-use, comprehensive series. It won't frustrate you by moving too fast, or let you get bored by moving too slow! You'll notice pics of many great performers; we added those to fire your imagination and help you stay focused on becoming a star yourself! To top it off, you can put what you learn to work when you play along with the companion CD. Set your sights high by beginning with BASIX™... the series that will get you there!

Cover photo: Paul Reed Smith

Alfred

10.50

TABLE OF CONTENTS

This book is a fast and fun way to learn how to use scales and modes from day one and will provide a strong foundation from which to build upon. Learning scales and modes and being able to identify their sounds will give you a better command of the fretboard. This approach to learning and organizing melodic material will greatly enhance your guitar prowess.

A lick is a pattern or series of notes that can be used as a basis for guitar soloing. *Basix™ Scales and Modes* will give you an understanding of the different scales and modes and how easily you can use them in your own playing.

Each chapter in this book has three sections. The first section describes the scale or mode, lists chords it works well with, musical styles it is most commonly used with and shows the intervals of the scale or mode. The second section shows the scales and modes, in most cases, in five different positions on the neck. The positions are shown in neck position, standard notation and tablature. The third section contains licks written in the style of famous guitarists well known for their use of a particular scale or mode.

This book will not only show you the different scales and modes but will show examples of how they are used in improvising solos.

All music has been written in both standard notation and in tablature to allow both the beginning and the experienced guitarist to take full advantage of this book.

TABLATURE EXPLANATION

Tablature is a system of notation that graphically represents the strings and frets of the guitar fingerboard. Each note is indicated by placing a number, which indicates the fret or finger position to be picked, on the appropriate string. For example:

4th String, 5th Fret

1st String, 10th Fret
2nd String, 10th Fret } Played together

An open G chord

DICTIONARY OF GUITAR NOTATION

Arpeggio

Arpeggio: Strike the notes of the chord shown from the bottom to top. Quickly release each note after striking.

Bends

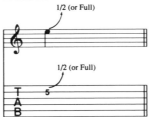

One- or Two-Note Up Bend: Pick the first note, then bend the string to sound up either one or two frets.

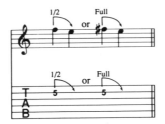

One- or Two-Note Down Bend: Pick the first (bent) note, then straighten the string to sound the lower (second) note.

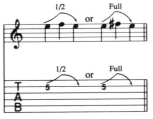

Pick Bend and Release: Pick the first note, bend the string up one or two frets to sound the higher (second) note, then straighten the string to sound the original (first) note again. Pick only the first note.

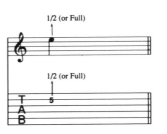

Bend and Then Pick: Bend the first note up one or two frets before picking it. This is usually followed by a down bend.

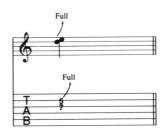

Unison Bend: Pick the lower (first) note slightly before picking the higher (second) note, but before picking the higher note, bend the string of the lower note so it matches the pitch of the higher note. These notes are always picked on adjacent strings.

Harmonics

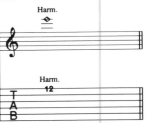

Natural Harmonic: The fre finger lightly touches the string over the fret, and the the string is picked. A chimelike sound is produced.

Artificial Harmonic: After the note is fretted normally the pick hand lightly touches the string at the fre (in parentheses) with one finger while plucking with another.

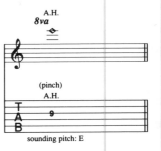

sounding pitch: E

Artificial "Pinch" Harmonic: After the note i fretted normally, add the edge of the thumb or the ti of the index finger to the normal pick attack to produce the harmonic. Hig volume or distortion will allow for a greater variety c harmonics.

Mutes

Muffled Strings: A percussive sound is produced by laying the fret hand across the strings without depressing them to the fretboard, and then striking the strings with the pick hand.

Palm Mute (P.M.): The note is partially muted by the pick hand by lightly touching the string or strings just before the bridge.

Slides

Slide: Pick the lower first note, then slide the fret finger up to sound the higher (second) note. The higher note is not picked again.

Slide and Pick: Same as the slide except the higher note is also picked.

Long Slide: Strike the note during the slide up to the desired note.

Slide Off: Same as the slide except the fret finger slides up or down an indefinite number of frets, removing the finger tension at the end of the slide.

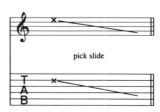

Pick Slide: The edge of the pick slides down the entire string. A scratchy, downward sound is produced.

Tapping

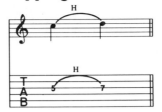

Hammer-on: Pick the lower (first) note, then hammer-on (tap down) the higher (second) note with another finger. Pick only the first note. These notes are always played on the same string.

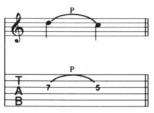

Pull-off: Place both fret fingers on the two notes to be played. Pick the higher (first) note, then pull-off (raise up) the finger of the higher note while keeping the lower note fretted. Pick only the first note.

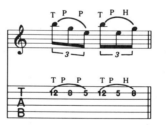

Tapping: Tap down on the fretted string with the index or middle finger of the pick hand. This is usually followed by a pull-off to sound the lower note.

Tremolos

Tremolo Picking: The string is picked down-and-up as rapidly as possible.

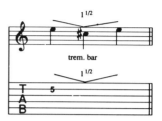

Tremolo Bar: A note or chord is raised or lowered a specified number of frets by pushing down or pulling up on the tremolo bar, and then returning to the original note or chord.

Vibrato

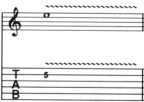

Vibrato: Pick the string as the fret finger or a tremolo bar rapidly rolls back and forth or bends up and down, making the note sound slightly higher and lower. An exaggerated vibrato can be achieved by rolling the fret finger a greater distance.

SCALE AND MODE DEFINITIONS

Scales

A set of notes with a particular arrangement of whole and half steps. Each scale has a different sound because of its unique arrangement of these intervals.

Modes

Modes are scales derived from the major and minor scales.

How To Use This Book

All scales, modes and licks are shown in the tonality of E to help show you how they relate to one another. Each scale is shown in five different positions on the neck. Using these you can play these scales anywhere on the neck and in any key. The note with the square around it is the root or tonic note, which in this book is E. To put these scales into other keys simply take the root note and move it, using the note chart, to the tonic or root of the key you wish to play in.

Note Chart

Number →	1	2	3	4	5	6	7	8	9	10	11	12	
String → E	F	F# Gb	G	G# Ab	A	A# Bb	B	C	C# Db	D	D# Eb	E	
B	C	C# Db	D	D# Eb	E	F	F# Gb	G	G# Ab	A	A# Bb	B	
G	G# Ab	A	A# Bb	B	C	C# Db	D	D# Eb	E	F	F# Gb	G	
D	D# Eb	E	F	F# Gb	G	G# Ab	A	A# Bb	B	C	C# Db	D	
A	A# Bb	B	C	C# Db	D	D# Eb	E	F	F# Gb	G	G# Ab	A	
E	F	F# Gb	G	G# Ab	A	A# Bb	B	C	C# Db	D	D# Eb	E	

Dave Pirner of Soul Asylum takes an emotional approach to his guitar playing—an attitude shared by many alternative rock guitarists of the 1980s and 90s.

Photo: Amy Lehman © 1995

MAJOR SCALE

Description

This scale is used as the basis from which many scales and modes are derived. This scale has a happy, upbeat, almost jubilant quality.

Chords

Major, Major Sevenths, Major Ninths, Elevenths

Musical Styles

Rock, Pop, Country, Jazz, Fusion

E MAJOR SCALE

Intervals

Root	2	3	4	5	6	7	Octave
	W	W	H	W	W	W	H

 Track 2

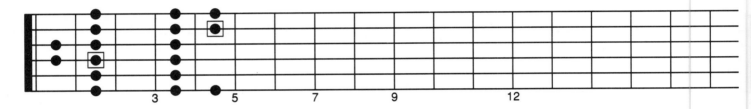

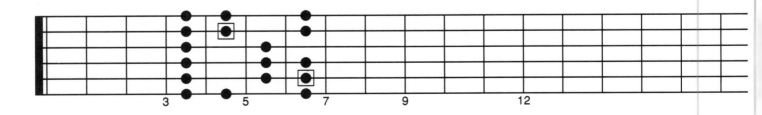

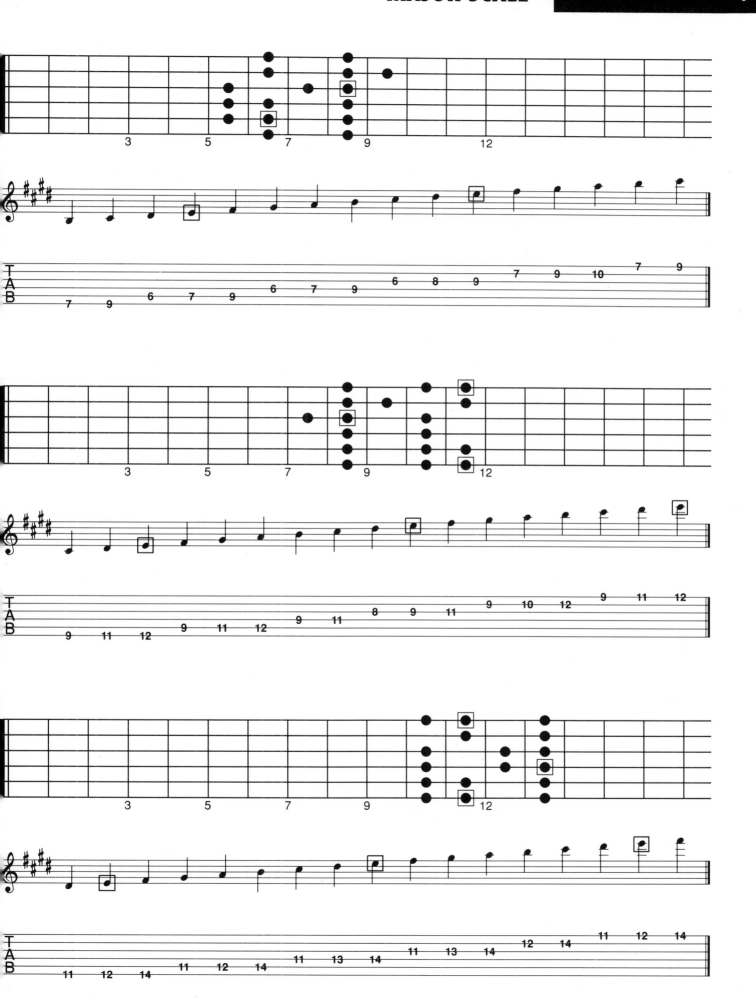

MAJOR LICKS IN THE STYLE OF...

ALEX LIFESON (RUSH) Track 3

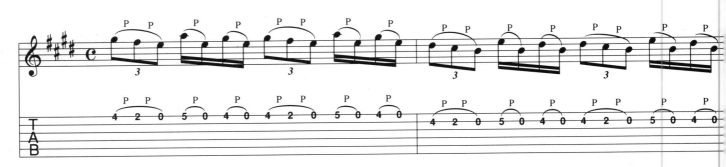

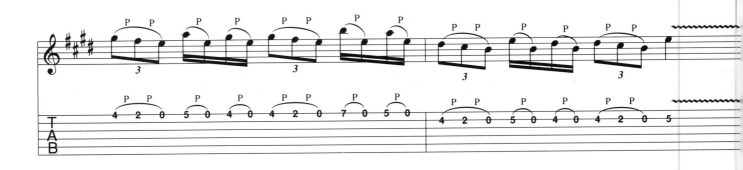

STEVE MORSE Track 4

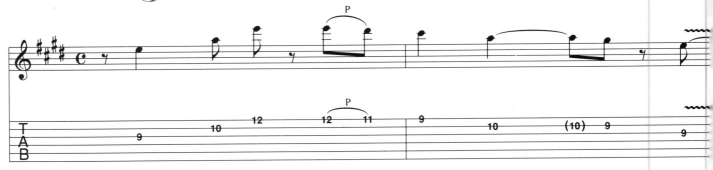

Rush continues to be popular because of the band's willingness to evolve musically. They have created a vast, layered sound more common in much larger groups, and Alex Lifeson's adventurous guitar playing has been a vital element of that sound.

DORIAN MODE

Description

This is the major scale with the third note and seventh note lowered 1/2 step. This jazz flavored mode has a sophisticated, soulful sound.

Chords

Minor, Minor Sevenths, Minor Ninths

E DORIAN MODE

E F G A B C D E

Musical Styles

Jazz, Fusion, Blues and Rock

Intervals

Root		2		♭3		4		5		6		♭7		Octave
	W		H		W		W		W		H		W	

 Track 5

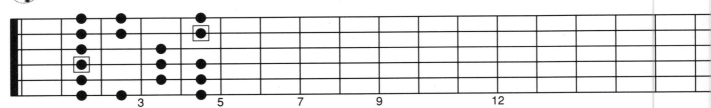

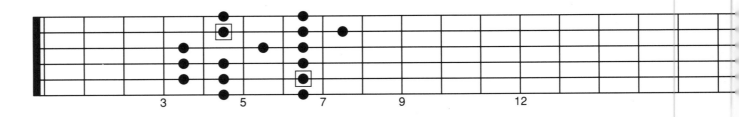

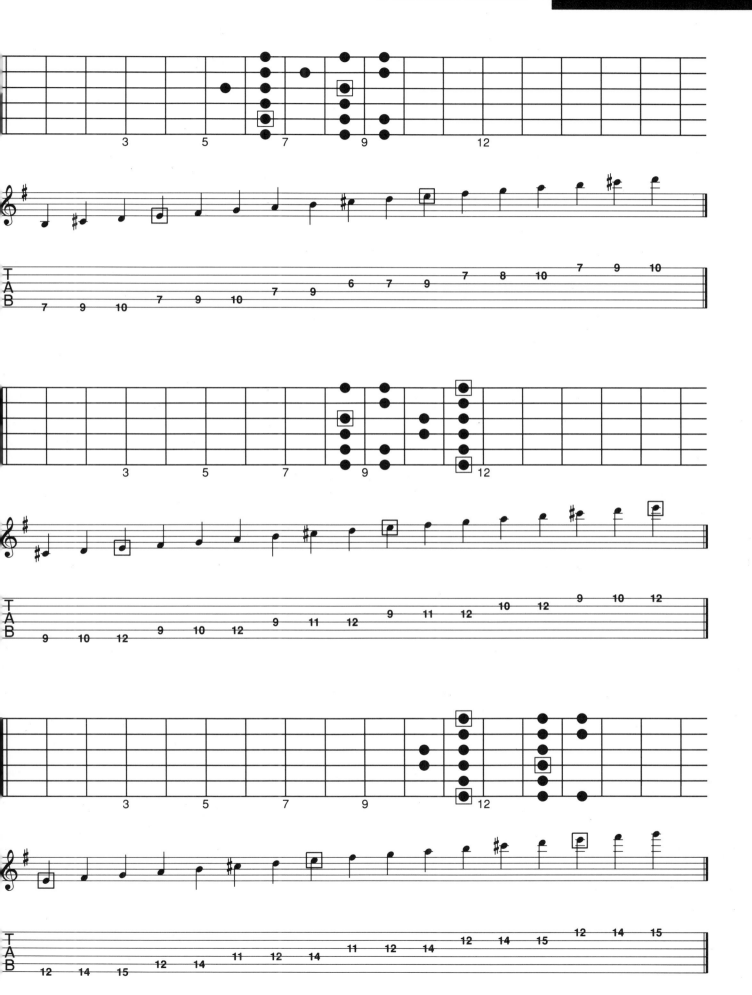

ERIC JOHNSON Track 6

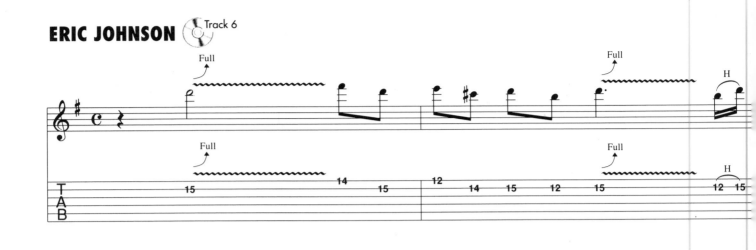

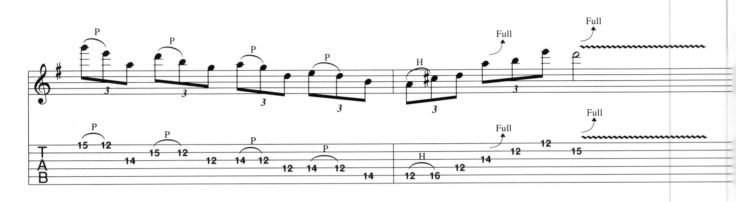

JOHN SCOFIELD Track 7

One of the new breed of guitar virtuosos, Eric Johnson took the music world by storm in the late 1980s, astounding guitar fans with a unique blend of speed, artistry and melodic improvisation.

Photo: Ken Settle

PHRYGIAN MODE

Description

This is the major scale with the second note, third note, sixth note and seventh note lowered 1/2 step. It is most commonly thought of as the flamenco mode, for its Spanish flavor. It is also often used by fusion and, strangely enough, speed metal players.

Chords

Major, Minor, Minor Sevenths

E PHRYGIAN MODE

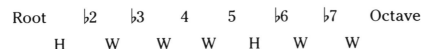

Musical Styles

Flamenco, Fusion, Speed Metal

Intervals

Root	♭2	♭3	4	5	♭6	♭7	Octave
	H	W	W	W	H	W	W

Track 8

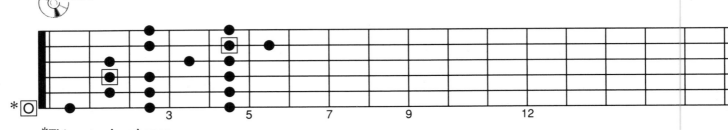

*This note played open

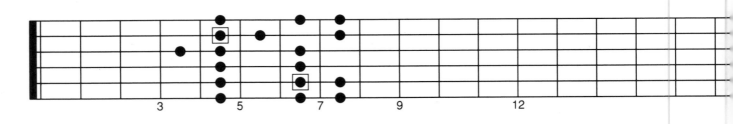

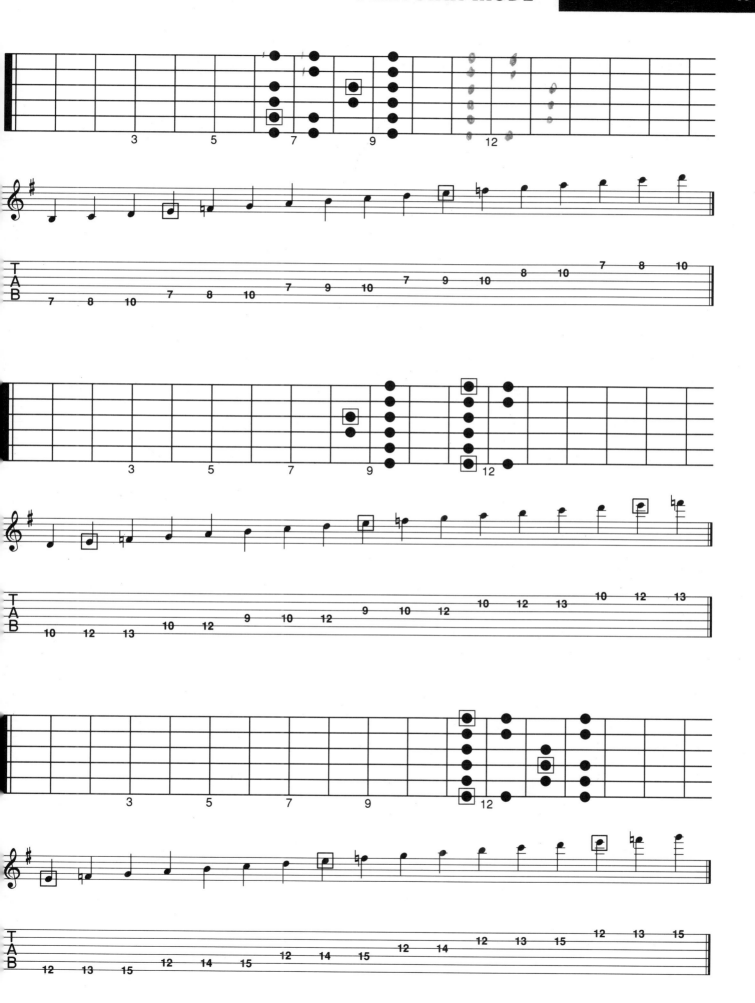

PHRYGIAN LICKS IN THE STYLE OF...

AL DI MEOLA  Track 9

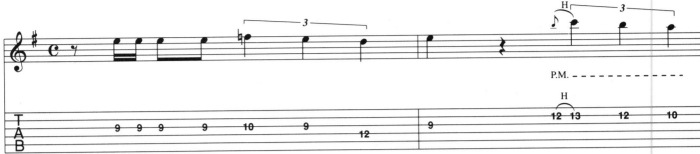

ALEX SKOLNICK (TESTAMENT) Track 10

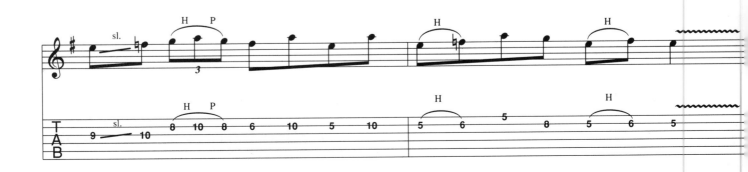

From his early work with Return to Forever to his own exciting solo career, Al DiMeola's technical ability and speed has inspired legions of jazz/rock guitarists.

Alex Skolnik

Though known for his pyrotechnic playing in the speed-metal band Testament, Alex Skolnick is equally adept in other musical styles, most notably jazz.

Photo: Ken Settle

LYDIAN MODE

Description

This is the major scale with the fourth note raised 1/2 step. This gives the scale an airy sound favored by the likes of Steve Vai, Eric Johnson, John Scofield and Scott Henderson.

Chords

Major, Major Sevenths, Major Ninths, Sharp Elevenths

E LYDIAN MODE

Musical Styles

Jazz, Fusion, Rock and Country

Intervals

Root		2		3		♯4		5		6		7		Octave
	W		W		W		H		W		W		H	

Track 11

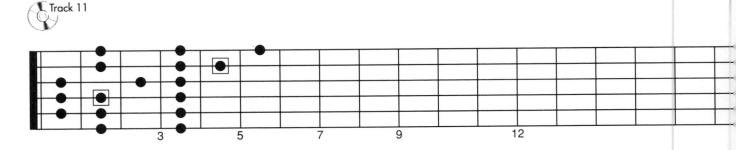

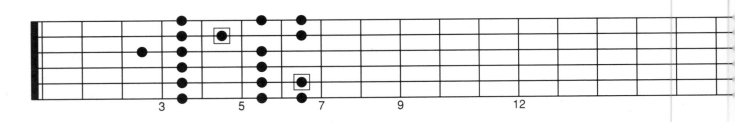

LYDIAN MODE

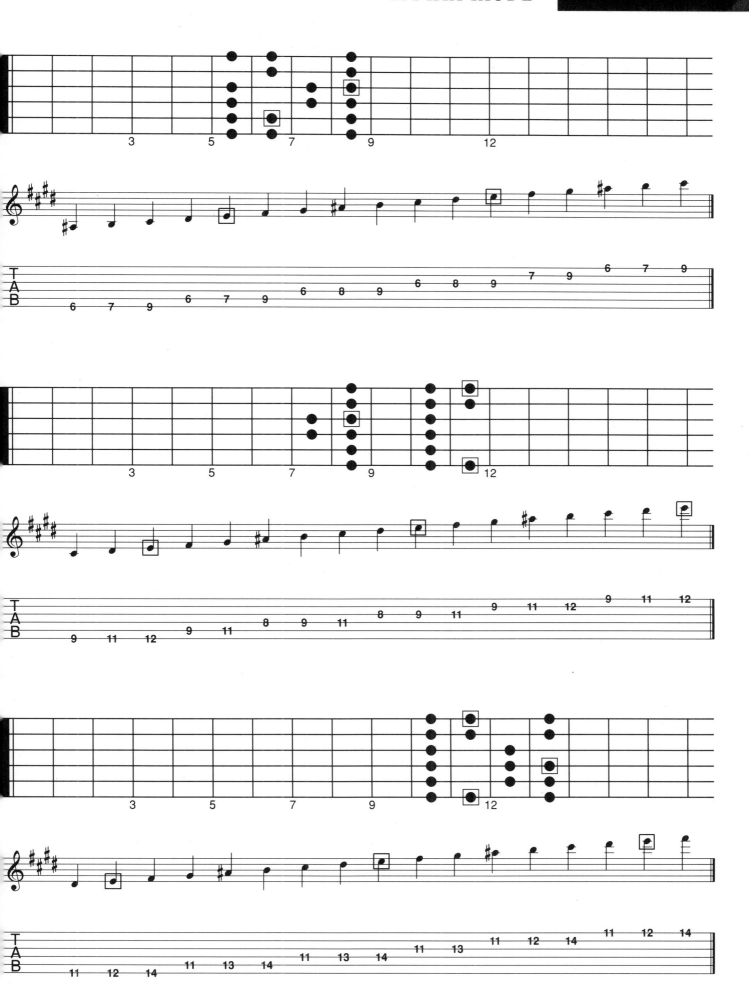

LYDIAN LICKS IN THE STYLE OF...

JOE SATRIANI Track 12

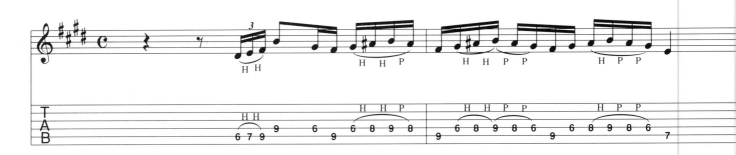

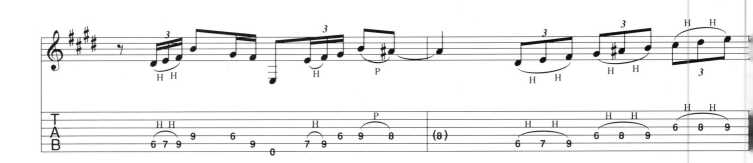

ALBERT LEE Track 13

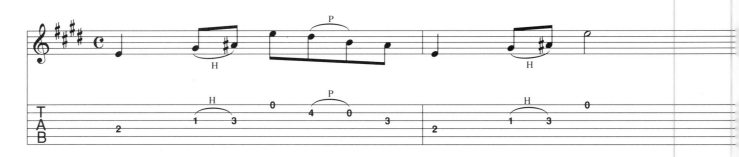

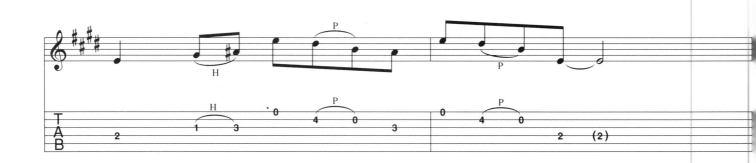

Photo: Glen La Ferman

*Called "the guitar player's guitar player," session player Joe Satriani has been
a mentor to the likes of Steve Vai, Larry Laloude (Primus) and many others.
His cutting-edge solo work has won him a devoted following as well.*

MIXOLYDIAN MODE

Description

This is the major scale with the seventh note lowered 1/2 step. This mode has a blues feel that also lends itself well to country and rockabilly.

Chords

Dominant Sevenths, Dominant Ninths

E MIXOLYDIAN MODE

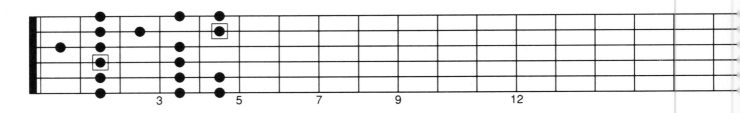

Musical Styles

Blues, Country, Rockabilly, and Rock

Intervals

Root	2	3	4	5	6	♭7	Octave
	W	W	H	W	W	H	W

 Track 14

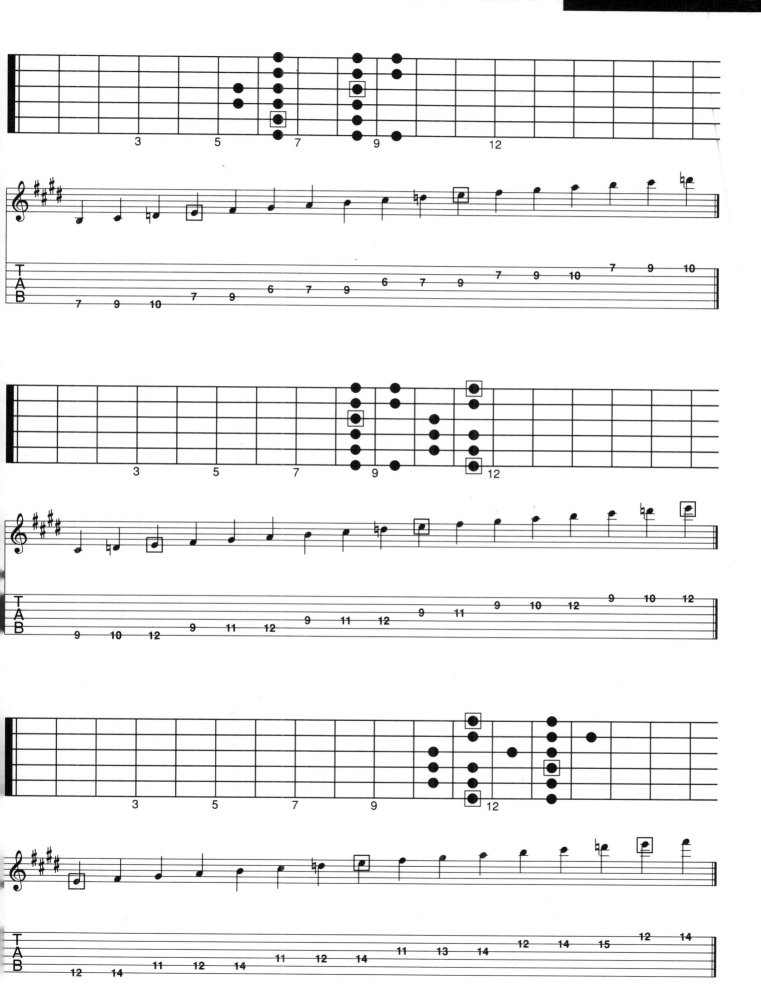

MIXOLYDIAN LICKS IN THE STYLE OF...

STEVIE RAY VAUGHN Track 15

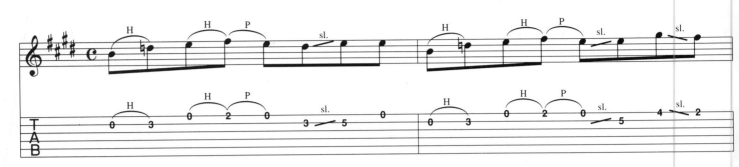

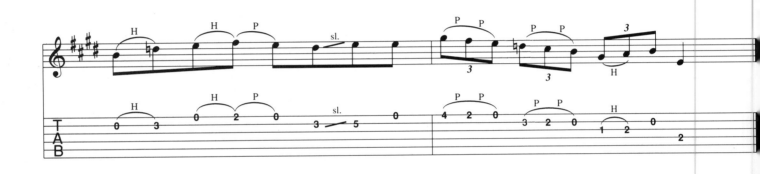

BILLY GIBBONS (ZZ TOP) Track 16

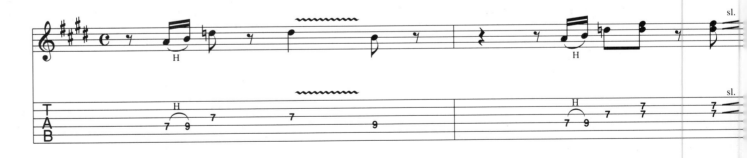

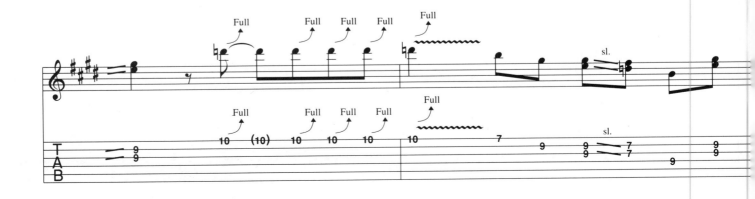

Billy Gibbons, the driving force behind ZZ Top, is an accomplished blues guitarist and has developed a unique sound and playing style that is widely imitated.

Photo: Ken Settle

LOCRIAN MODE

Description

This is the major scale with the second note, third note, fifth note, sixth note and seventh note lowered 1/2 step. This mode has a sinister sound that is mostly used by jazz players.

Chords

Minor Seventh Flat Fives

E LOCRIAN MODE

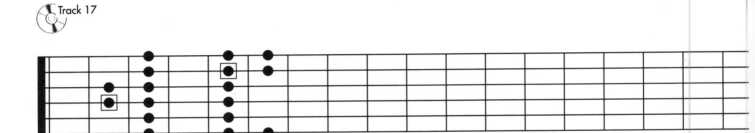

Musical Styles

Jazz and Fusion

Intervals

Root	♭2	♭3	4	♭5	♭6	♭7	Octave
	H	W	W	H	W	W	W

Track 17

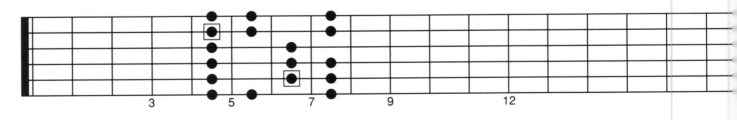

LOCRIAN MODE

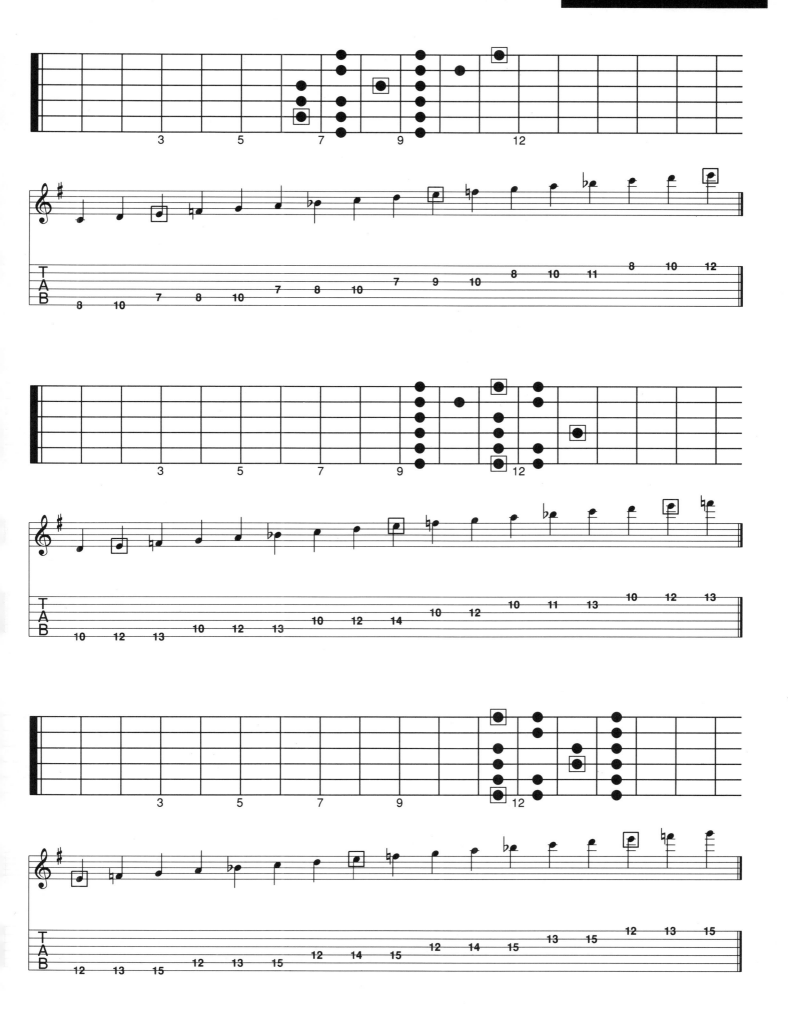

LOCRIAN LICKS IN THE STYLE OF...

ALLAN HOLDSWORTH Track 18

KIRK HAMMETT (METALLICA) Track 19

British guitarist Allan Holdsworth has pushed the boundaries of guitar playing, both with the progressive rock band UK, as well as with his own solo career. Eddie Van Halen is among his many fans.

NATURAL MINOR SCALE

Description

This is the saddest of all scales, and is used in many different styles of music to express sorrow and pain. It is also known as the Aeolian mode, and is one of the most often used scales in Western music.

Chords

Minor, Minor Sevenths, Minor Ninths

Musical Styles

Pop, Blues, Rock, Heavy Metal, Country and Fusion

Intervals

E NATURAL MINOR SCALE

Root	2	♭3	4	5	♭6	♭7	Octave
	W	H	W	W	H	W	W

 Track 20

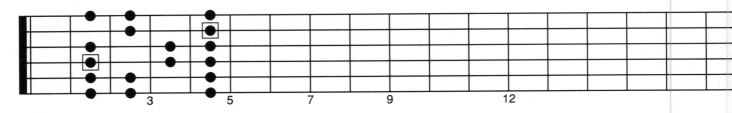

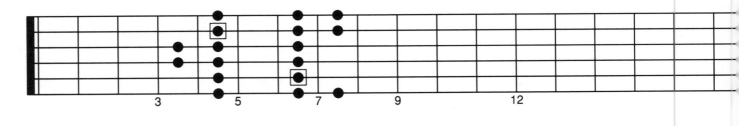

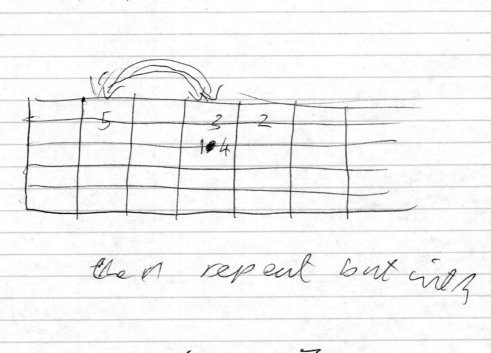

then repeat but with

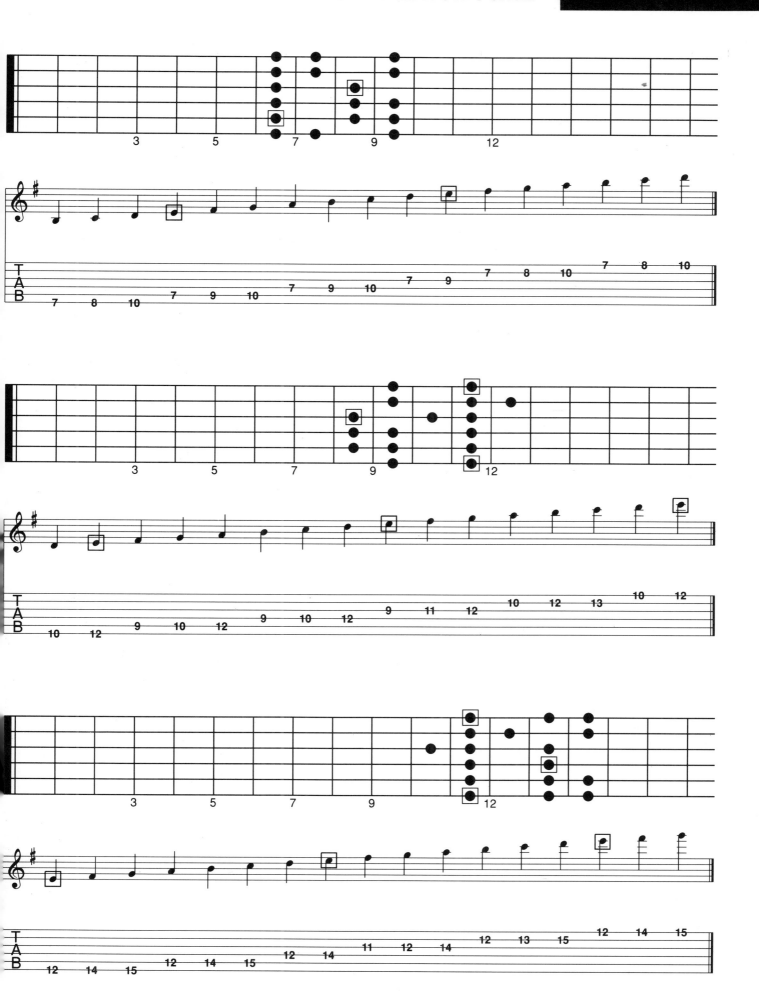

NATURAL MINOR LICKS IN THE STYLE OF...

Robben Ford is a multifaceted technician who can play both blues and jazz with equal confidence. His recordings with people like the great jazz trumpeter and innovator Miles Davis have inspired many young jazz guitarists.

HARMONIC MINOR SCALE

Description

This scale has an unusual sound that is very popular in classical music, most particularly the Baroque period. It is favored by classically influenced rock and heavy metal musicians.

Chords

Minor, Minor (Major Sevenths), Major Fifths (power chord)

E HARMONIC MINOR SCALE

Musical Styles

Classical, Rock, Heavy Metal and Jazz

Intervals

Root	2	♭3	4	5	♭6	7	Octave
W	H	W	W	H	W+H	H	

Track 23

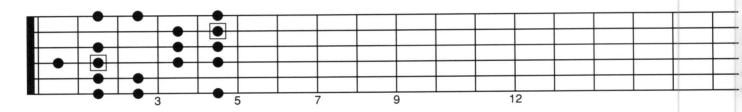

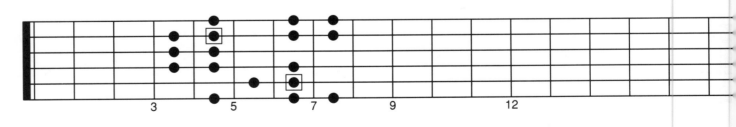

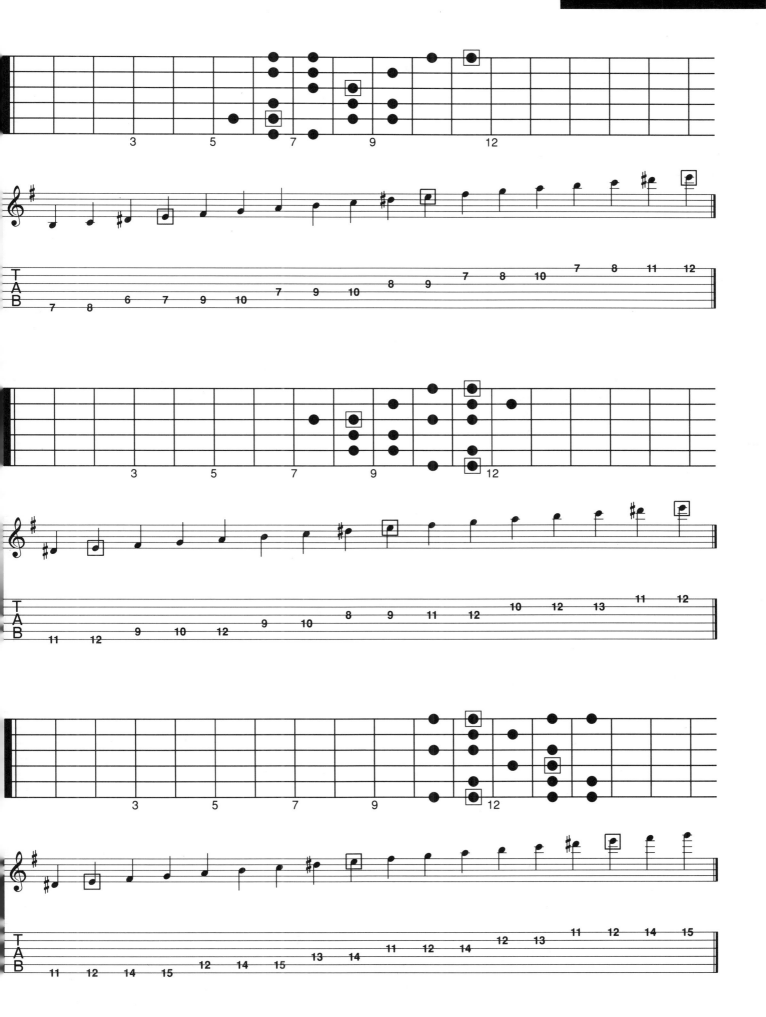

YNGWIE MALMSTEEN  Track 24

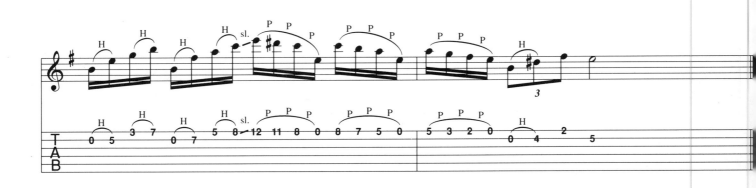

RANDY RHOADS  Track 25

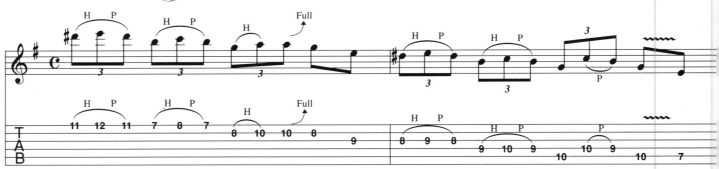

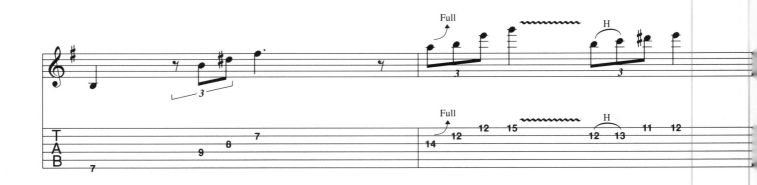

Randy Rhoads, whose brilliant career was cut tragically short with a fatal plane crash,
became familiar to most heavy metal fans when he joined Ozzie Osbourne's first solo band.

Photo: Star File Photos

MELODIC MINOR SCALE

Description

This is commonly known as the jazz minor scale. It is very useful in that it has qualities of both major and minor scales which express a wide range of emotions.

Chords

Minor, Minor (Major Sevenths), Minor Sixths

E MELODIC MINOR SCALE

Musical Styles

Jazz

Intervals

Root	2	♭3	4	5	6	7	Octave
	W	H	W	W	W	W	H

 Track 26

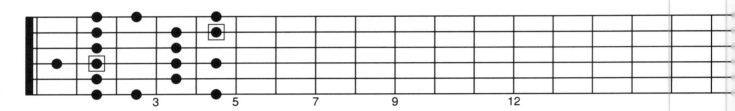

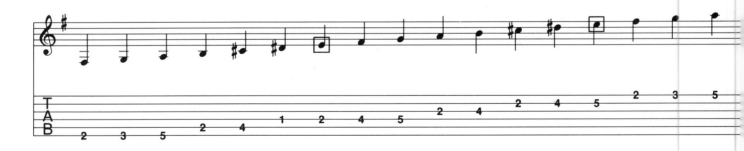

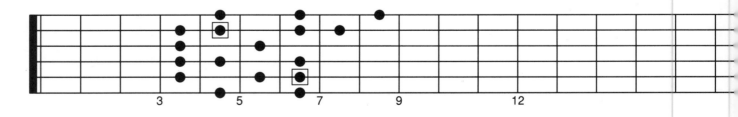

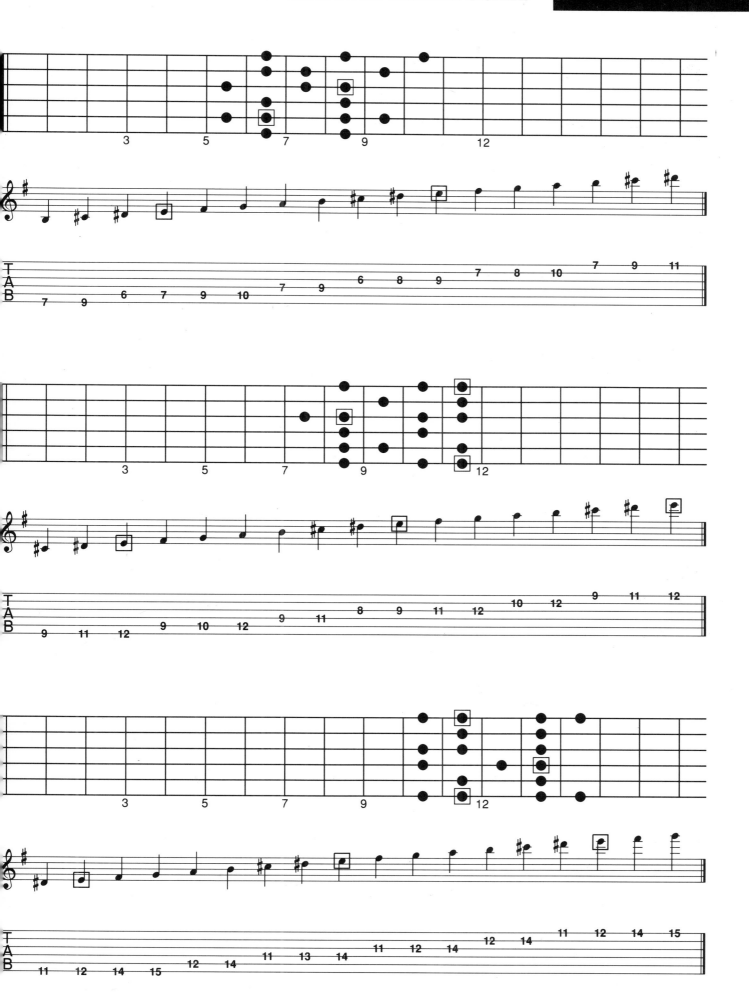

MELODIC MINOR LICKS IN THE STYLE OF...

JOE PASS  Track 27

MARK WHITFIELD Track 28

Joe Pass was the consummate jazz session guitarist. His playing can be heard on countless great recordings, and his smooth, fluid technique remains the standard to which many contemporary players aspire.

Photo: Institute of Jazz Studies

WHOLE TONE SCALE

Description

This is a scale constructed of tones a whole step apart, which keeps it from being anchored to any pitch. This lack of tonal center gives the scale a dreamlike floating quality.

Chords

Dominant Seven Flat Fives, Augmented

E WHOLE TONE SCALE

Musical Styles

Jazz, Fusion and Contemporary Classical

Intervals

Root	2	3	#4	#5	♭7	Octave
	W	W	W	W	W	W

 Track 29

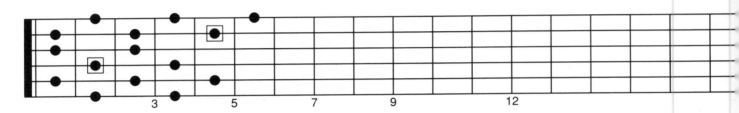

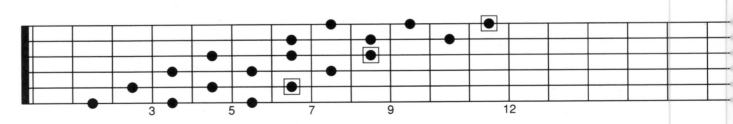

VERNON RIED (LIVING COLOR) — Track 30

ALLAN HOLDSWORTH — Track 31

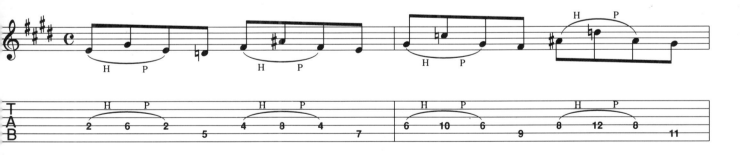

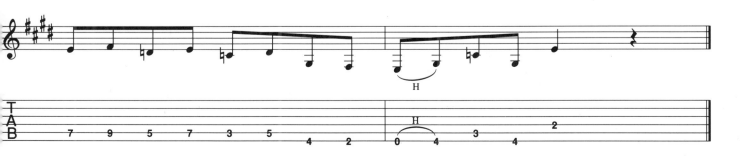

DIMINISHED SCALE

Description

This is an important jazz scale because it works well with altered seventh chords and chord extensions popular in this style of music. In heavy metal it is used over the flat five power chord which gives it an almost Gothic sound.

Chords

Diminished Sevenths, Minor Seventh Flat Fives, Dominant Seventh Flat Nines

E DIMINISHED SCALE

Musical Styles

Jazz, Fusion, Heavy Metal and Blues

Intervals

Root		2		♭3		4		♭5		♭6		♮6		7		Octave
	W		H		W		H		W		H		W		H	

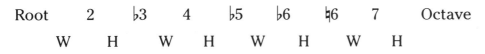

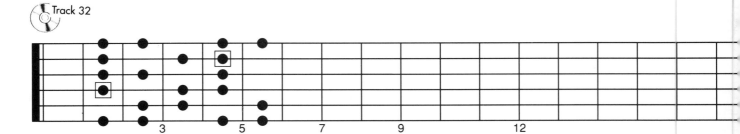

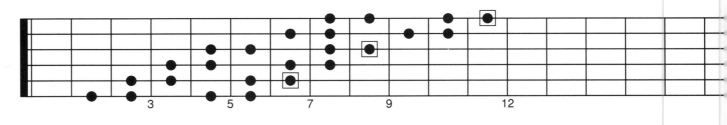

DIMINISHED LICKS IN THE STYLE OF...

SCOTT HENDERSON Track 33

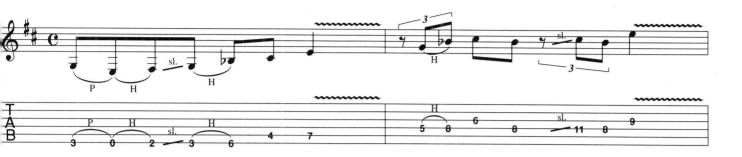

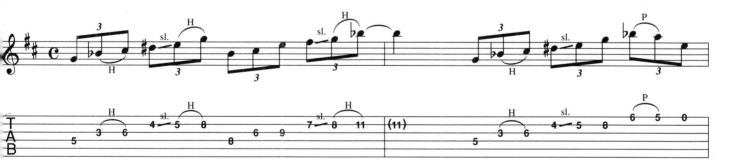

GEORGE LYNCH Track 34

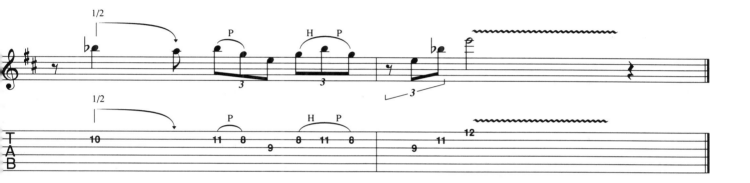

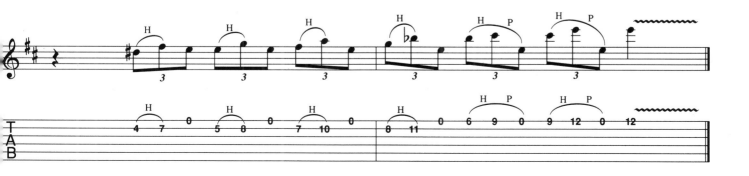

MAJOR PENTATONIC SCALE

Description

The pentatonic scale dates back thousands of years, and is still one of the most used today. The major pentatonic has a bright sound which lends itself well to country music.

Chords

Major, Major Sevenths, Dominant Sevenths

E MAJOR PENTATONIC SCALE

Musical Styles

Country, Blues, Fusion, Jazz and Rock

Intervals

Root		2		3		5		6		Octave
	W		W	W+H		W		W+H		

Track 35

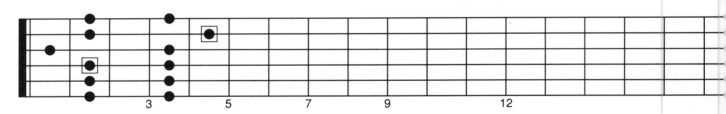

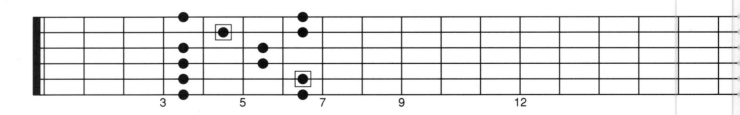

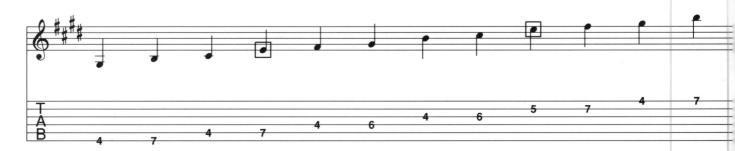

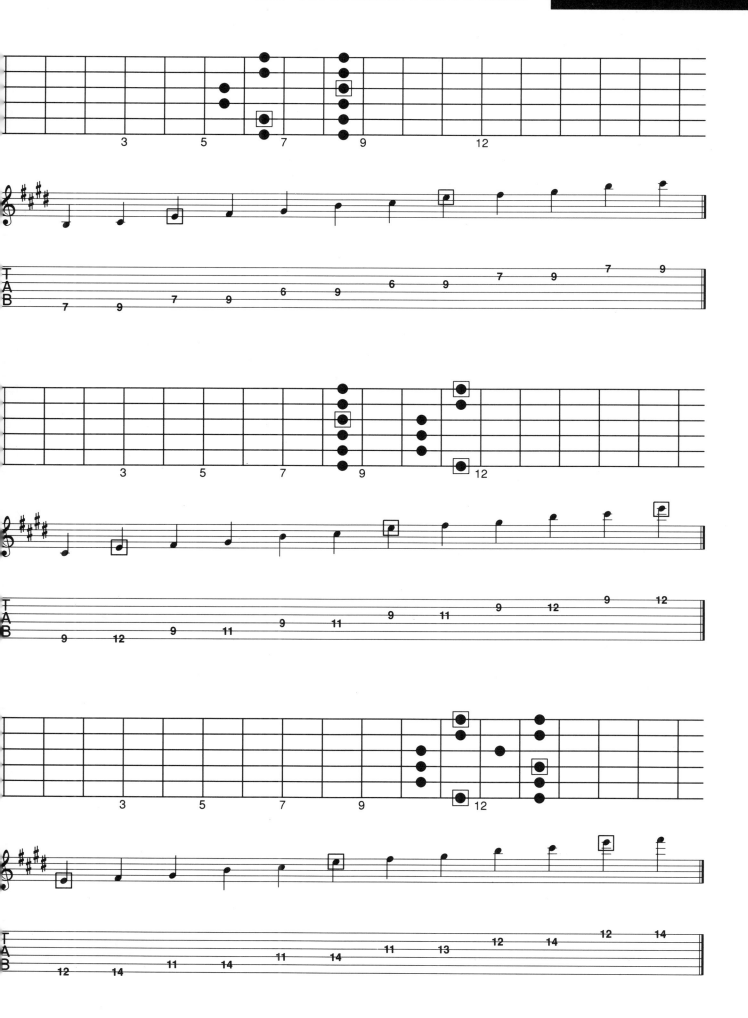

MARK KNOPFLER (DIRE STRAITS) Track 36

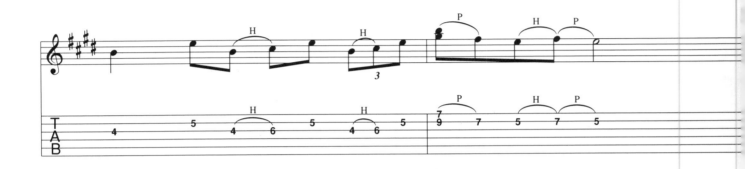

JIMI HENDRIX Track 37

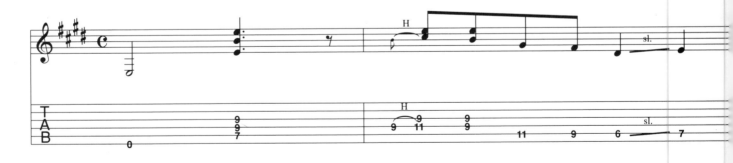

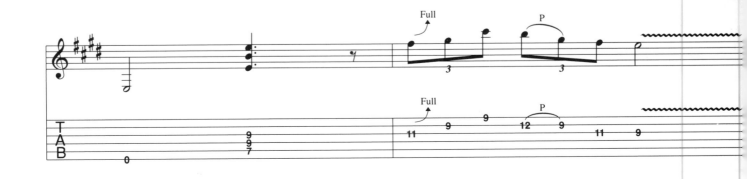

Perhaps more than anyone who ever picked up a guitar, Jimi Hendrix discovered the widespread sonic capabilities of the instrument. He was a true pioneer, and retains a legendary status for his revolutionary guitar work.

MINOR PENTATONIC SCALE

Description

This bluesy sounding scale is by far the most used in blues and rock. One of the reasons for this is because when played over most common blues and rock chord progressions, this scale leaves a small margin for error.

Chords

Minor, Minor Sevenths, Dominant Sevenths

Musical Styles

Rock, Blues, Heavy Metal, Fusion and Jazz

Intervals

Root	♭3	4	5	♭7	Octave
W+H	W	W	W+H	W	

E MINOR PENTATONIC SCALE

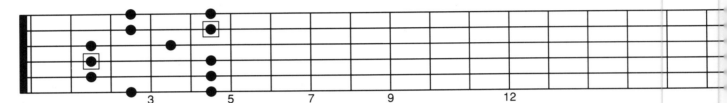

 Track 38

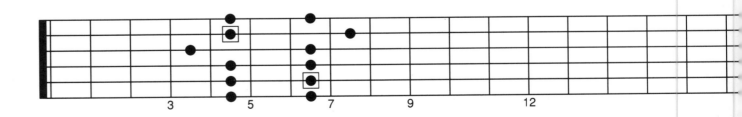

ANGUS YOUNG (AC DC) — Track 39

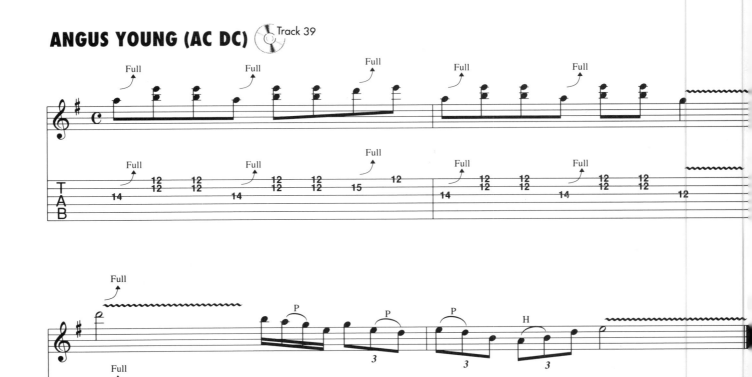

NUNO BETTENCOURT (EXTREME) — Track 40

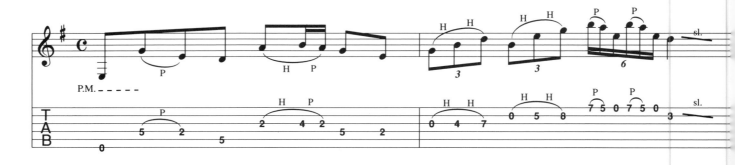

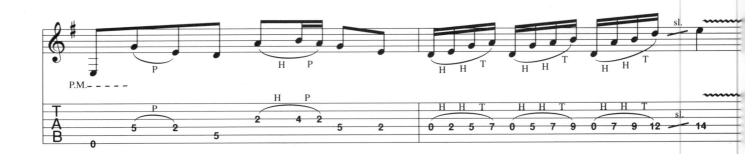

As lead guitarist of AC/DC, *Angus Young* has spent three decades making traditional blues riffs sound fresh and powerul in ways no one else imagined.

BLUES SCALE

56

Description

This is the minor pentatonic with the addition of one note, the raised fourth, which gives it a uniquely blues sound.

Chords

Major Fifths, Dominant Sevenths, Dominant Ninths, Minor Sevenths, Minor Ninths

Musical Styles

Blues, Rock, Jazz and Fusion

E BLUES SCALE

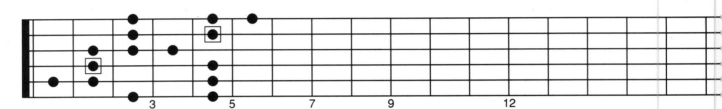

Intervals

Root	♭3	4	♯4	5	♭7	Octave
	W+H	W	H	H	W+H	W

 Track 41

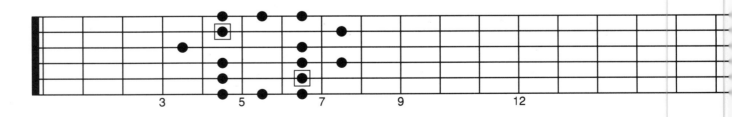

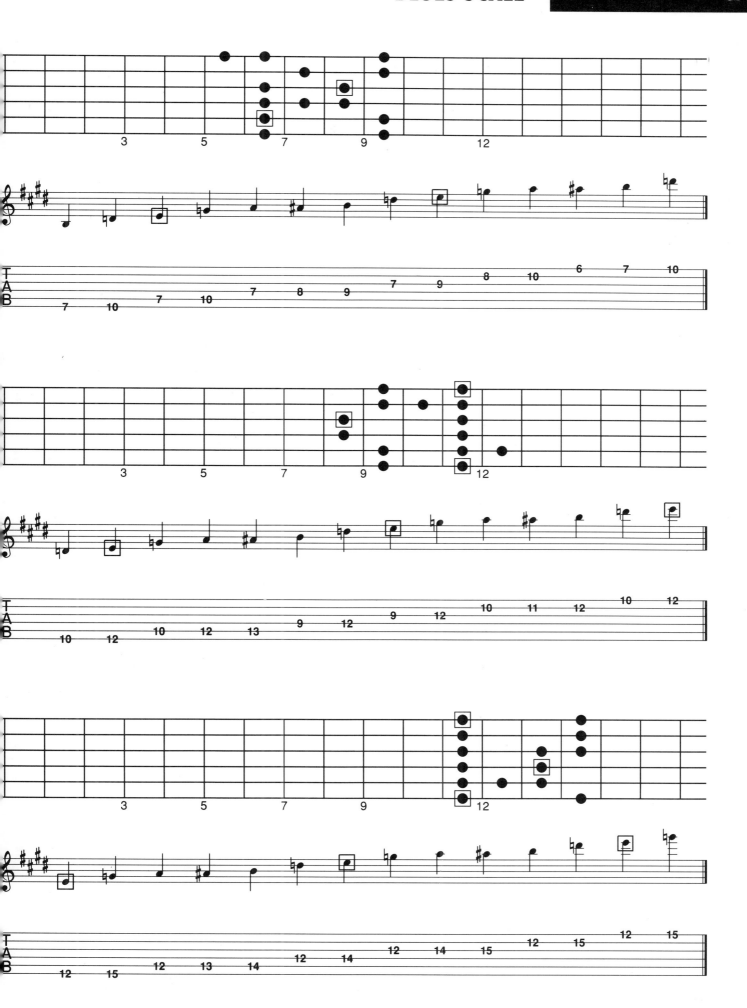

ERIC CLAPTON 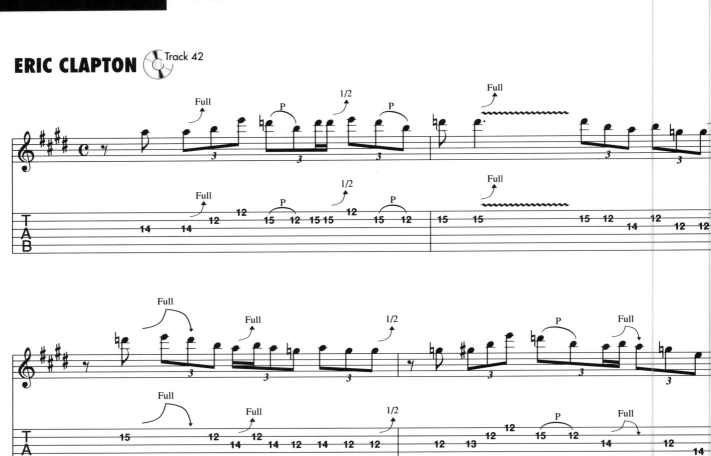 Track 42

B. B. KING  Track 43

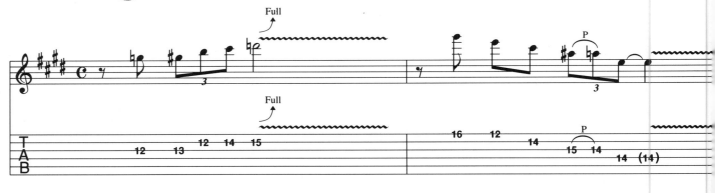

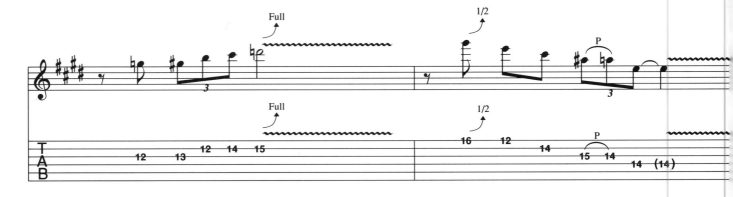

*Like Jimi Hendrix, Eric Clapton is a true rock icon. From his early
work with* Bluesbreakers *and* The Yardbirds, *to the legendary
supergroup* Cream *and his own solo career, Clapton's influence
can be heard in most contemporary rock music.*

In this section we are going to show you two extended solos using different combinations of scales and modes. We will cite the different scales and modes as they are used. This should help demonstrate how you can use them in your own playing. Try combining different scales and modes on your own as they are the key to all solos.

ROCK Track 44

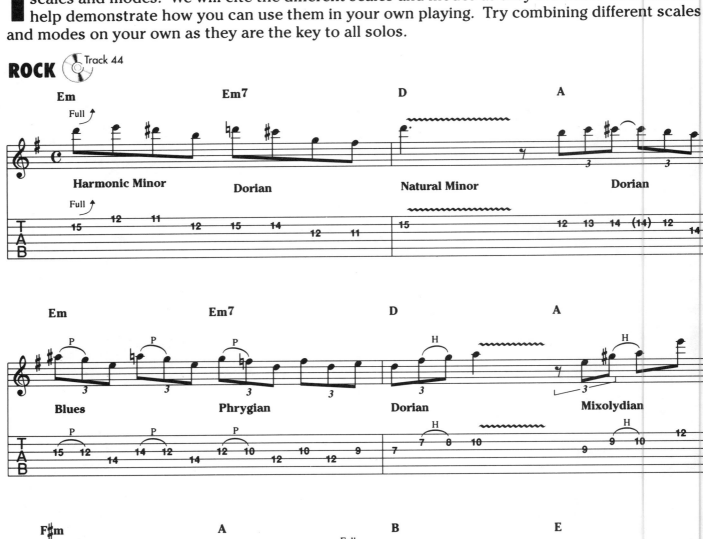

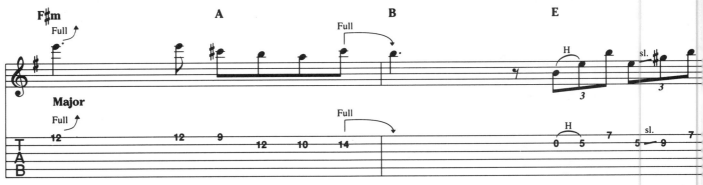

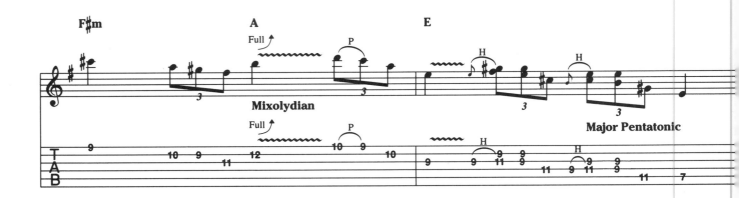

The Police *was one of the most popular bands of the 1980s, and inventive guitarist Andy Summers was the perfect complement to Steward Copeland's lively drumming and Sting's bass lines and soaring vocals.*

BLUES  Track 45

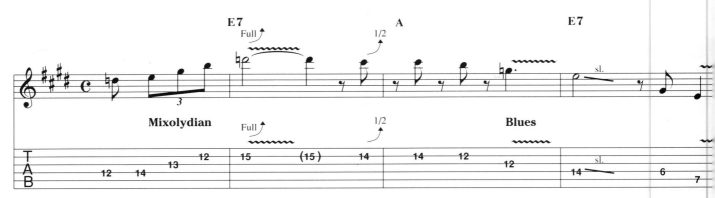

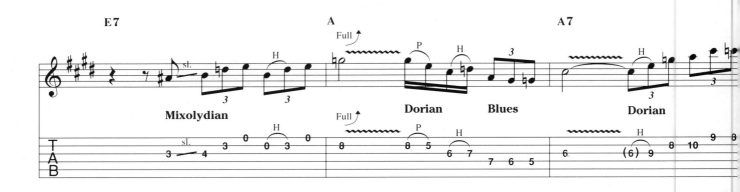

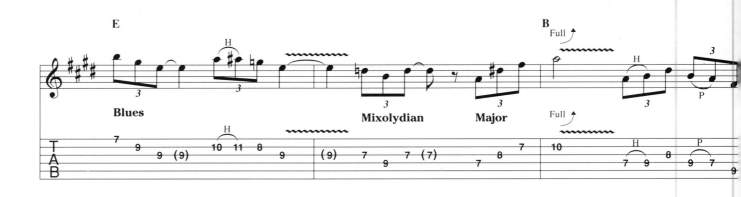

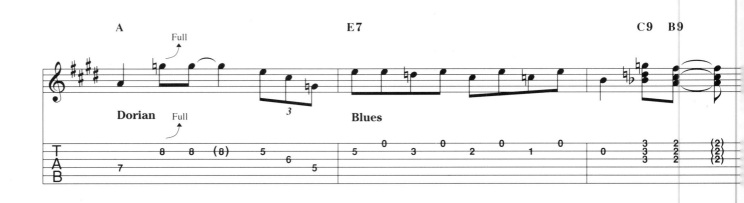

Stevie Ray Vaughn amazed fans with his unique approach to the blues. His playing displayed a new level of technical brilliance while losing none of the soulful emotional edge.

Guitar Fingerboard Chart
Frets 1–12